PUFFIN BOOKS

The Day Our Teacher Went Batty

Gervase Phinn is a teacher, freelance lecturer, author, poet, educational consultant, school inspector, visiting professor of education and, last but by no means least, father of four. Most of his time is spent in schools with teachers and children.

He is the author of *The Other Side of the Dale*, *Over Hill and Dale*, and *Head Over Heels in the Dales*. His first poetry collection, *It Takes One to Know One*, is also available in Puffin.

Also by Gervase Phinn

IT TAKES ONE TO KNOW ONE

For older readers

THE OTHER SIDE OF THE DALE
OVER HILL AND DALE
HEAD OVER HEELS IN THE DALES

Gervase Phinn

The Day Our Teacher Went Batty

Illustrated by Chris Mould

PUFFIN BOOKS

PUFFIN BOOKS

Published by the Penguin Group
Penguin Books Ltd, 80 Strand, London WC2R 0RL, England
Penguin Putnam Inc., 375 Hudson Street, New York, New York 10014, USA
Penguin Books Australia Ltd, 250 Camberwell Road, Camberwell, Victoria 3124, Australia
Penguin Books Canada Ltd, 10 Alcorn Avenue, Toronto, Ontario, Canada M4V 3B2
Penguin Books India (P) Ltd, 11 Community Centre, Panchsheel Park, New Delhi – 110 017, India
Penguin Books (NZ) Ltd, Cnr Rosedale and Airborne Roads, Albany, Auckland, New Zealand
Penguin Books (South Africa) (Pty) Ltd, 24 Sturdee Avenue, Rosebank 2196, South Africa

Penguin Books Ltd, Registered Offices: 80 Strand, London WC2R 0RL, England

www.penguin.com

'Classroom Creatures', 'School Trip', 'Book Week', 'Class Discussion', 'The Little Chatterbox', 'Bible
Class', 'My Teacher', 'Christmas Presents for Miss', 'Parents' Evening', 'Interrogation in the Nursery',
'Poetry Lesson', 'Farmgirl', 'Asking Questions', 'Mr Lee Teaches Poetry' and 'Once Upon a Time'
first published in Classroom Creatures, by Roselea Publications, 1996
'It Takes One to Know One', first published in Crack Another Yolk, edited by John Foster, by Oxford
University Press, 1996

This collection published 2002
1

Text copyright © Gervase Phinn, 2002
Illustrations copyright © Chris Mould, 2002
All rights reserved

The moral right of the author and illustrator has been asserted

Set in 12/16 Joanna

Made and printed in England by Clays Ltd, St Ives plc

British Library Cataloguing in Publication Data
A CIP catalogue record for this book is available from the British Library

ISBN 0–141–31445–1

Contents

Nativity Play

Oh, Miss, I don't want to be Joseph,
Miss, I really don't want to be him,
With a cloak of bright red and a towel on my head
And a cotton wool beard on my chin.

Oh Miss, please don't make me a shepherd,
I just won't be able to sleep.
I'll go weak at the knees and wool makes me sneeze
And I really am frightened of sheep.

Oh Miss, I just can't be the landlord
Who says there's no room in the inn.
I'll get in a fright when it comes to the night
And I know that I'll let Mary in.

Oh Miss, you're not serious – an angel?
Can't Peter take that part instead?
I'll look such a clown in a white silky gown,
And a halo stuck up on me head.

Oh Miss, I am not being a camel!
Or cow or an ox or an ass!
I'll look quite absurd and I won't say a word,
And all of the audience will laugh.

Oh Miss, I'd rather not be a Wise Man,
Who brings precious gifts from afar.
But the part right for me, and I hope you'll agree,
In this play – can I be the star?

Question and Answer

'And where did you go on holiday this year, Richard?'
Asked the teacher.
'We went to Mablethorpe, Miss,'
The little boy replied.
'And did you go on a donkey?'
Asked the teacher.
'Oh no, Miss,'
The little boy replied,
'On a bus!'

Exam

An angry sun glared through the high window.
The hall was stifling and stuffy,
And we were wet with sweat and breathless,
Sweltering in our seats, sizzling,
Wilting in the heat,
Glued to the paper with sticky hands.
All was quiet, all was still,
Save for the teacher's gentle snoring.
He has fallen asleep at his desk.

Truth Will Tell

A small child was splashing poster paint
On a great grey piece of paper.
'Do you paint a picture every week?'
Asked the school inspector.

The small child shook his little head.
'Hardly ever as a rule,
But Miss said we've got to paint today –
There's an important visitor in school!'

Infant Nativity

He looked like a little angel,
With his round eyes as blue as the sky,
And an innocent, childlike expression.

He peered through the curtains at the assembled parents,
Dressed in his white silk costume trimmed with silver,
And waited for his entrance.

He turned to his friend and whispered:
'If Miss thinks I'm being a flipping snowflake next year,
She's got another think coming!'

Dinner Time

The important visitor smiled widely.
The infant munched and crunched his biscuit
And stared with wide, unblinking eyes.

The important visitor said:
'My little boy demolishes food like a dinosaur too.'
The infant replied between bites:
'He eats raw meat then, does he?'

Parents Like You to:

Watch your manners,
Be polite,
Tidy your room,
Switch off the light,
Wash the dishes,
Polish your shoes,
Brush your teeth,
Watch your p's and q's,
Kiss your auntie,
Never swear,
Eat your greens,
Comb your hair,
Do your homework,
Go to sleep,
Set the table,
Wipe your feet,

Flush the toilet,
Sweep the path,
Change your socks,
Have a bath,
Sit up smartly,
Stand up straight,
Blow your nose,
Clean your plate,
Hang your coat up,
Close the door,
Say 'please' and 'thank you',
Be in by four . . .

And generally behave as they think they did
when they were our age !

Less Able

He could not describe the beauty that surrounded him:
The soft green dale and craggy hills.
He could not spell the names
Of those mysterious places which he knew so well.
But he could snare a rabbit, ride a horse,
Repair a fence and dig a dike,
Drive a tractor, plough a field,
Milk a cow and lamb a ewe,
Name a bird with a faded feather,
Smell the seasons and predict the weather,
That less able child could.

Clear English

Mr Smart our English teacher
Stood at the board one day.
He turned and said: 'Put pencils down,
And kindly look this way.
Before you leave the school next week
And in the world a job you seek,
Remember that at interview
Be clear in what you say.
I've put some notes upon the board
But firstly want to say a word.

Now, you will not achieve success
If hair and clothes are in a mess.
And if you wear a grubby shirt
And your old shoes are caked in dirt,
The outcome of the interview
I am sure you all can guess.

Well, this applies to English too.
They'll think you haven't got a clue
If over words you stop and stumble,
Whisper, wince and mouth and mumble,
Become confused and start to stutter,
Stare at the floor and merely mutter,
They certainly won't pick you.
So – always choose your words with care
Speak clearly or you'll rue it,
Now everyone look at the blackboard please
And then I will go through it.'

Last in the Queue

When they gave out the instruments at school,
I was the last in the queue.
There were trumpets and trombones,
French horns and flutes,
Violins and violas,
Clarinets and cornets,
Guitars and saxophones,
Euphoniums and bassoons,
Tubas and cellos,
Drums and piccolos and oboes.

There was only the double bass left for me,
And the trouble is, I'm four foot three!

A Proper Poet

Today we have a real-live poet in school –
This gentleman who's standing next to me.
I must say when I met him in the entrance,
He was not as I imagined he would be.

I'd always thought that poets were tall and wan,
With eyes as dark and deep as any sea,
So when I saw this jolly little man,
He didn't seem a proper poet to me.

The poets I've seen in pictures dress in black
With velvet britches buttoned at the knee,
So when I saw the T-shirt and the jeans,
He didn't look a proper poet to me.

I've read that famous poets are often ill,
And die consumptive deaths on a settee.
Well, I'd never seen a healthier-looking man,
He just didn't look a proper poet to me.

My favourite poems are by Tennyson and Keats.
This modern stuff is not my cup of tea,
So when I heard our poet was keen on rap
He didn't sound a proper poet to me.

Well, I'm certain that we'll all enjoy his poems
And listen – after all we've paid his fee –
I hope that they're in verses and they rhyme,
For that is proper poetry – to me.

Uncle Eric

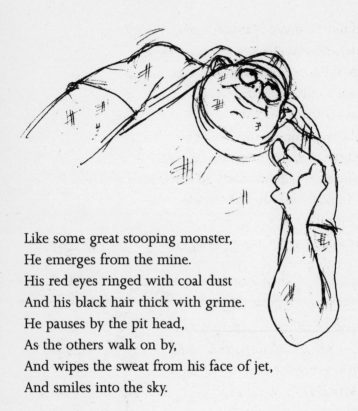

Like some great stooping monster,
He emerges from the mine.
His red eyes ringed with coal dust
And his black hair thick with grime.
He pauses by the pit head,
As the others walk on by,
And wipes the sweat from his face of jet,
And smiles into the sky.

School Visitor

Good morning, Mr Manning,
Do please take a chair.
A cup of tea is on its way,
Are you comfortable there?
I must say that your letter
Caught me unprepared.
The children are so nervous,
And the staff – quite frankly – scared.
Now I think you'll find the pupils here
Really try their best.
The reading's good, the writing's neat,
Feel free to give a test.
I know this is a little school
But we do strive for perfection.
I must say that we've never had
A thorough school inspection . . .
Oh, you're not the school inspector,
And Manning's not your name.
You came about the toilets,
And the caretaker's blocked drain.

Sister Says

When Richard clambered up the tree
And fell to earth and grazed his knee,
Sprained his ankle, scraped his shin,
Cracked his elbow, cut his chin,
His sister said, as she stood by:
'I didn't know that boys could fly!'

One winter's day, when on his sledge,
Matthew hit a hawthorn hedge,
Scratched his face, bruised his hip,
Thumped his nose and split his lip.
His sister said: 'I didn't know
That boys liked rolling in the snow!'

When Dominic, on his roller skates,
Collided with the garden gates,
Blacked his eye, banged his head,
Stubbed his toe and broke a leg,
His sister was heard to announce:
'I didn't know that boys could bounce!'

The Teacher

The teacher (it is sad but true)
Likes telling children what to do.
At college he is taught to shout,
And learns to order kids about.
With nerves of steel and fists of iron
He strides the classroom like a lion,
Then freezes with an icy stare,
And throws his hands up in the air,
And shakes his head in deep despair.

The teacher (it is fair to say)
Likes giving orders every day.
She can't speak quietly at all,
But has to shriek and scream and bawl,
Bellow, bark and screech and huff,
Holler, wail and pant and puff,
Lament, complain and sigh and drone,
Yell and yelp and roar and moan,
Grimace, grunt and growl and groan.

The teacher (yes, I hear you sigh)
Does not use words like you and I.
In training for his tough profession
He learns each teacher-like expression:
 'Stop fiddling, boy, and pay attention
Or you will join me in detention!'
'I really don't know why I bother,
In one ear and out the other . . .'
'I'm waiting, Class . . .' 'My, my, you're slow, . . .'
'I'm not here for my health, you know!'
'Now settle down and look this way,'
And 'You, girl, put that thing away!'
'Take out your books . . .' 'What did I just say?'

As soon as teachers enter college
They cram their minds with all this knowledge.
Then they emerge completely changed.
It's very odd, it's very strange,
And that is why (it's sad but true),
That teachers aren't like me and you.

Little Philosopher

'Your writing's so untidy,'
Matthew heard his teacher moan.
'I know, Miss,' said the pupil,
'This pen has a life of its own!'

Bonfire Night Blues

Remember, remember,
The fifth of November,
Gunpowder, treason and plot.
Well, after last week's washout,
I would rather not.
My *Roman Candle* spluttered
And refused to light the sky.
My *Sparklers* wouldn't sparkle
And my *Rockets* wouldn't fly.
My *Bangers*, they just would not bang
And my *Golden Rain* went phutt!
My *Whizz-bang* blew out clouds of smoke
And covered me in soot.
My *Thunderflash* just fizzed a bit,
My *Crackers* wouldn't light.

My *Silver Fountain* whimpered –
It was such a sorry sight.
My *Jumping Jacks* declined to jump
And my *Catherine Wheels* to turn.
Not a single flipping firework worked,
Then the bonfire wouldn't burn.
I was feeling really cold and wet,
But when I began to groan,
My dad got really angry,
And he told me not to moan.
He said I was like a big damp squib
And then he sent me home.
So I don't want to remember Bonfire Night this year!

The Lucky Horseshoe

Dad found a rusty horseshoe in the garage
on the floor, He said that it would bring
us luck if placed above the door.
So he climbed high up the ladder to
nail the horseshoe in,
But, dropped the heavy hammer, which
cracked him on the chin.
It clattered down towards the ground, but when it
reached the floor
It bounced back like a boomerang and
smacked him on the jaw.
Down it went a second time, rebounding
off his shin,
Then bounced back up, and once again it
cracked him on the chin.
Down came the nail and iron shoe,
rebounding off his head
Then Dad fell off the ladder and
bruised his arms and leg.
Such was his fate, he lay prostrate, I thought
that he was dead.
Then came a moan and then a groan.
'What rotten luck!' he said.

Epitaph

Underneath this mound of clay
There lies a teacher (some might say).
Her name was Miss Euphemia Grey,
Who to her class had much to say
And beat her pupils every day.
She ruled them with an iron fist –
Now sadly gone but gladly missed.

Out Fishing

A heron,
Needle-beaked,
Bright-eyed,
Barrel-chested,
Silver-feathered,
Stands in the river,
Spiking fish,
Then swallowing them whole –
Effortlessly.

A boy
Sits on the bank,
Holding his rod
Above the weedy water,
Watching the float,
Waiting for a bite –
Patiently.

A Parent's Prayer

Always believe in yourself.
Promise always to be compassionate.
Appreciate that you make mistakes,
Recognize that I do too.
Entrust me with your worries.
Never doubt that I will support you when you need me.
Talk to me about the things you find difficult.
Share your dreams.

Please understand that I can have moods just like you.
Receive a little advice now and again.
Accept that I sometimes get things wrong.
You need to help me to get things right.
Enjoy your life.
Realize that I love you without reservation.

Rhyme-time

Our teacher, Mrs Paradigm,
To teach us children how to rhyme,
Has asked us all to take our name
And find a word that sounds the same.
And so we did.

Andy is dandy,
Bhupa is super,
Kitty is pretty and
Clare is fair.
Mable is able,
Scott is hot,
Luke is cute but
Danuta is cuter.
Dwight is bright,
Trevor is clever,
Terry is merry and
Jim is slim.
Brenda is tender,
Cecil is special,
Dean is keen but
Rowena is keener.

Liz is a whizz,
Danny is canny,
Pip is hip and
Gill is brill,
Holly is jolly,
Grace is ace,
Pete is sweet but
Nita is sweeter.
Kate is great,
Mick is quick,
Nancy is fancy and
Paul is tall.
Sally is pally,
Wendy is trendy,
Dave is brave but
Fraser is braver.

The trouble is my name is Matt,
And I can't think of a rhyme for that.
Well, not a nice one anyway!

Pageboy

At my sister's wedding
I was a pageboy dressed in blue,
With little velvet trousers
And a buckle on each shoe.

I had to wear white stockings
And a massive pink bow tie,
And a really silly frilly shirt.
I thought that I would die.

With everybody watching,
I shuffled down the aisle,
With a silver horseshoe in my hands,
And a really stupid smile.

'You do look very handsome,'
My doting mother said.
I looked at her and then replied,
'I wish that I were dead!'

'Well, I think you look nice,' she sighed,
'And very, very cute,
In your pink bow tie and buckled shoes
And your little pageboy suit.'

'Well, thank you very much,' I said,
Glaring at my mother,
'But I am twenty-one years old,
And my sister's elder brother!'

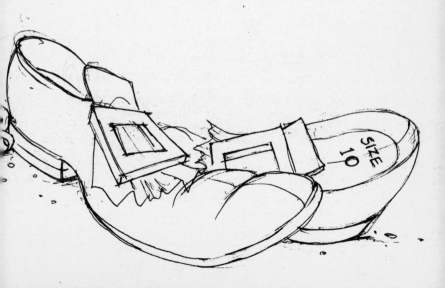

The Parent's Warning

If you clamber on that frame,
And bang your head just once again . . .
Don't say I didn't warn you!

If you tumble from that tree,
Scrape your elbow, graze a knee . . .
Don't say I never told you so!

If you stumble on that ledge,
And fall and break both your legs . . .
Don't come running to me.

Signs of the Times

I sometimes stop and stand and stare
In silent incredulity,
At signs and labels everywhere
Which show Man's blind stupidity.

In a newspaper: 'Man battered in fish shop!'
On a can of paint: 'For indoor and outdoor use only.'
By a motorway: 'Attention! All cats' eyes have
been removed!'
On a hairdryer: 'Do not use while sleeping.'
In a shop: 'Bargain basement upstairs.'
On a packet of peanuts: 'Warning! This product
contains nuts.'

At a station: 'Beware of moving trains.'
At the fair: 'Ears pierced while you wait.'
On a bottle of sleeping pills: 'Warning:
May cause drowsiness.'
In a supermarket: 'Our staff are here to
serve you.' On an examination paper:
'This option is compulsory.'
In a gym: 'If you cannot read these
instructions, ask for help.'
On a child's toy: 'Please note, this gun
does not fire real bullets.'
In a public toilet: 'Wet floor!
This is not an instruction.'

Dominic

Of all the children I have known,
There's none who is so accident prone
As Dominic, who, it's fair to say,
Has accidents nearly every day.
He's trapped his fingers in the door,
Trod on crabs near the salt sea shore,
Dived like Tarzan from a tree,
Cut his head and grazed a knee.
Poked a pencil up his nose,
Dropped an iron on his toes.
He spilt a scalding cup of coffee,
Choked on a slab of sticky toffee.
He's tumbled, sleeping, from his bed,
Broke an arm and bruised a leg.
Doctors and nurses all agree
There's none so accident prone as he.
Yet, when from hospital he comes home,
Dominic doesn't cry and moan
He says, 'How boring life would be
If you didn't have an interesting son like me!'

Accident

When I knocked a plate off the table
And it shattered on the floor,
And the food spattered across the wall,
Dad raised the roof with a roar.
'For goodness sake, be careful!
I've told you so before!'

When Dad knocked a mug off the table
And tipped it over the chair,
And the coffee spattered across the wall,
Dad growled like a grizzly bear.
'For goodness sake,' he shook his head,
'Who left the coffee there?'

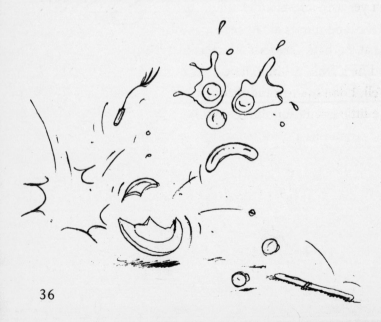

The Inspector Calls

The room was cold and dingy
And the windows far from clean.
No sand or clay, no wall display,
Not a book was to be seen.

'I am sure you have a lot of fun,'
The school inspector said,
To the rows of nervous children
Who sat in silent dread.

'I am sure you have a lot of fun,'
The visitor repeated,
And the children nodded obediently,
'Oh yes sir,' they all bleated.

But at the back sat David,
And he shook his little head.
'Well, I don't have a lot of fun,'
The little infant said.

'Of course you do!' the teacher snapped,
And fixed him with a glare.
'We're always having lots of fun!'
In a voice that said: 'Beware!'

But David shook his head again,
And they heard the infant say:
'Well, I do not remember it –
I must have been away that day!'

Will You Come to My Party?

Will you come to my party?
Oh please say that you will come.
There'll be lots to eat and lots to drink
It really will be fun.

The philosopher observed: 'I'll think about it.'
The musician trilled: 'Sounds good to me.'
The psychologist thought it a mad idea.
The butler said: 'I'll wait and see.'
The psychologist replied that she'd bear it in mind.
The meteorologist said, 'Fine.'
The greengrocer remarked that he'd weigh things up.
The horologist would 'if I have the time.'
The insomniac sighed she'd sleep on it.
'I'm sorry,' the penitent said.
The optician concluded: 'It looks all right.'
The librarian said: 'Take it as read.'

The cardiologist hadn't the heart to refuse.
The wrangler whooped: 'Yippee!'
The inventor declared: 'I can make it, all right.'
The escapologist said: 'If I'm free.'
The fisherman told me he'd drop me a line.
The rugby player promised he'd try.
The campanologist said: 'I'll give you a ring.'
The examiner asked me: 'Why?'
The parachutist said that he might drop in.
The informer that he'd let me know.
'I'd love to come!' the fiancée cried.
The killjoy answered, 'No!'
The wrestler growled he would put it on hold.
The rambler said: 'I'm on the way.'
'Oh, I'll be there,' the naturist said,
'I've nothing on that day.'

Conversation with the Infant

'You look so deep in thought,'
The school inspector said.
'Now tell me please, my little man,
What is going through your head?'

'Well, have you ever stopped to think,'
The little infant said,
'That when I'm twenty-one years old,
You'll probably be dead!'

What's What?

Watch it!
Watch what?
Just watch it, see!
See what?
You know what!
What?
You're asking for it!
Asking for what?
That does it!
Does what?
You're in for it now!
In for what?
What's what, that's what!
Oh.
Do I make myself clear?
Perfectly.

I Would Sooner

I would sooner:

Kiss a witch with a wart on her chin,
Live for a week in a smelly dustbin,
Wrestle an octopus underwater,
Play Postman's Knock with Dracula's daughter,
Stand in a cellar in the cold and dark,
Swim in the sea with a great white shark,
Eat a plate of worms on toast,
Spend all night with a headless ghost,
Tickle a tarantula's hairy leg,
Sleep with a slug in a slimy bed,
Walk in a wood when the moon shines bright,
Go through the graveyard at dead of night,
Dance with a dragon in his dusty lair,
Play blind man's buff with a grizzly bear.

Than:

Get on the wrong side of my teacher
when she's in a bad mood!

Conversation with the Teacher

Richard!
Yes, Miss?
I think I can see a coat on the floor
Getting dusty and dirty and trampled upon.
Yes, Miss, so can I!

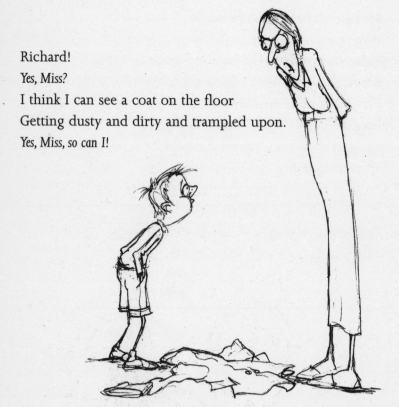

Conversation with the School Inspector

Would you read to me?
Why?
Because I would like you to.
Why?
Because I would like to hear how well you read.
Is it your hobby?
No, it's my job.
Funny sort of job!

Bonfire Night

I remember my first Bonfire Night.
It was cold and clear and the air smelled of smoke.
My father sat me high on his shoulders to see
the dancing flames
And the red sparks spitting in the air.
My face burned with the heat.
And then I saw him –
The figure sitting on the wigwam of wood.
I screamed and screamed and screamed.
'There's a man on top,' I cried, 'a man in the fire!
Oh help him, Daddy, please!'
And everyone laughed.
'It's just the guy,' my father said.
'He's made of rags and paper.
He's not real.'
But I was sad and scared to see
Those clinging fingers of fire
Scorch the stuffed body, crackling the arms,
Those searing tongues of flame lick round
the bloated legs,
And swallow up the wide-eyed, smiling face.

Now, as I stand around the bonfire,
My own child perched high on my shoulders,
I recall my father's words:
'He's just a guy. He's made of rags and paper.
He's not real.'
Yet, still I shudder at the sight of the blazing figure
Burning in the night.

7.

The Day Our Teacher Went Batty

On April Fool's Day
Miss Stanley emerged from the storeroom
And, between finger and thumb,
She held something black and rubbery
    with two small gleaming eyes.
'Very funny,' she said, smiling and holding up
    the creature for us all to see.
'And who,' asked our teacher, 'is the prankster?
Who put this plastic toy bat in my cupboard?'
When no one answered, Miss Stanley asked again:
'The April Fool is over now, so come along,
    so we can start our writing.'

Still no one said a word.
'Jason Thompson, was it you?
I see you smirking at the back.
If you expect me to scream, you will be disappointed.'
And then the creature turned its black and furry head,
And flapped its rubbery wings,
And showed a set of sharp and shiny teeth.
It was no toy the teacher held.
The bat had fluttered in through the skylight
And slept in the storeroom in the dusty dark,
Until disturbed by the teacher.
The corridors echoed with Miss Stanley's screams
That April Fool's Day.

Love Poem

The big black bull called to the cow
As she happily munched on the hay:
'O beautiful bovine,' he bellowed out loud,
'I love you, my dear Charolais.
Come into my field and how happy we'll be
Together, oh what do you say?'
The cow, she looked up and replied with a smile,
'I'm not in the mooo-d today.'

The big white ram called to the sheep,
As she happily munched the grass,
'O exquisite ovine,' he bleated out loud,
'You're my bonny, my black-faced lass.
Your eyes are so large and your wool is so fine
Together how happy we'll be.
Please say you'll be mine, you beautiful sheep,
For ewe are the one for me.'

Day Out

At the cinema,
Little Richard
Pushed a piece of popcorn up his nose.
'What's wrong?' asked Dad.
'Why are you wriggling about in your seat?
Sit still and watch the film.'
'I've got a piece of popcorn up my nose,' sniffed Richard.
'What!' cried Dad.
'Shush!' said the man behind.
'Shush!' said the woman in front.
'I've got a piece of popcorn up my nose,'
whispered Richard.

In the toilets,
Dad asked:
'How did you manage to get a piece of
popcorn up your nose?'
'I don't know,' snuffled little Richard, 'I just pushed it up.'
'You are a very silly boy,' said Dad.
'Blow your nose!'
So little Richard blew and blew on
his handkerchief,
But with no success.
Dad poked and probed,
Prodded and pinched,
But the piece of popcorn would not come down.

At the hospital,
Dad told the doctor:
'He's got a piece of popcorn up his nose.'
The doctor shook his head and smiled,
And poor, sad Richard, he began to cry.
'Don't worry, little man,' said the doctor gently,
'I'm very good at popcorn up people's noses.'
He produced a little torch,
And some long, long, silver tweezers.
'Head back, eyes closed, keep still,' he said,
And there, in his hand, was the piece of popcorn.

At home,
Mum asked Dad:
'Did you both have a nice time?'
'No!' snapped Dad.
'Richard pushed a piece of popcorn up his nose.
We had to go to hospital.'
Mum shook her head and smiled.
'Are you all right, Richard?' asked Mum.
'Fine,' said Richard, smiling.
'What happened to the popcorn?' she asked.
'Oh that,' little Richard replied. 'I ate it.'

A Father's Advice to His Son

Always smile at those you meet,
And they will do the same.
Look for good in others, son,
And don't waste time on blame.
Never be ashamed of crying,
It's not a sign you're weak.
Don't be quick to criticize,
And think before you speak.
Give more than you take, my son.
Do no one hurt nor harm.
Don't be afraid of being wrong,
And always chance your arm.
Stick firmly to your principles,
Don't follow fads and trends.
And always answer to your heart,
And value all your friends.
Keep that sense of humour,
It will help you to survive,
And don't take life too seriously, son,
For none comes out alive.

Asking Questions

Have you cleaned your teeth?
Have you washed your neck?
Have you combed your haystack hair?

Have you cleaned your shoes?
Have you washed your hands?
Have you changed your underwear?

Is your homework done?
Is the hamster fed?
Have you put your bike away?

Have you closed the gate?
Have you tidied your room?
Have you read your book today?

My parents sound inquisitive people,
They ask an awful lot of questions.
But they don't really expect me to answer them,
They just ask!

With Bells On

Now, if you are all looking this way, children, I am going to tell you the story of Christmas.

I've heard it, Miss.

Yes, I know that you have heard it, Briony, we have all heard it, dear, and we are all going to hear it again.

Why, Miss?

Because we are. It's a very special story, so special, in fact, that it is well worth repeating. Now, sit up smartly, children, nice straight backs, eyes this way, and we will begin. It was a cold, cold winter night many, many years ago when Mary and Joseph arrived in Bethlehem. Joseph walked ahead, holding up his lamp to light the way.

Didn't he have a torch, Miss?

No, Kimberley, he didn't have a torch. There were no torches in those days. Mary was on an old donkey which walked oh so slowly. Clip-clop, clip-clop he went. I think he knew that he was carrying a very precious burden that night.

Miss, we live next door to Mrs Burdon.

This is a different burden, Patrick. This burden was a very heavy weight.

Mrs Burdon's very heavy, Miss. My mum says she's fat.

Patrick, dear, just listen. This story has nothing to do with Mrs Burdon. As I was saying, Mary was on an old donkey which walked oh so slowly. Clip-clop, clip-clop he went.

Miss, I went on a donkey this year at Blackpool. It ran off along the sands and my dad had to chase it. It kicked my dad and tried to bite him, Miss.

Yes, well, this donkey was a very special donkey, Dean,
a very gentle donkey.

Did it have bells on, Miss?

No, it didn't have bells on.

Didn't they have bells in those days, Miss?

I'm sure they did have bells, Dean, but this donkey didn't
have any.

The donkey I went on at Blackpool had bells on.

Yes, well, this one didn't, Dean. Now, Mary knew she was
going to have a baby very soon. She had been travelling
all day and she felt very very tired.

Miss, my dad was very very tired after he chased the donkey.

Mary was tired because she had been travelling all day and
was having a baby.

Miss, my Auntie Brenda felt very very tired when she was having my cousin Oliver. She had swollen ankles and a bad back and, Miss, she was always being sick. She said it was the last baby she was going to have because . . .

Patrick, just listen, dear. Mary and Joseph had been waiting so long for the arrival of their very special baby.

Nine months!

That's right, Patrick. My goodness, you do know a lot about babies.

Miss, I know where babies come from as well. My dad told me.

Yes, well, this is not the time nor the place to go into that.

Did she go to the hospital, Miss?

No, she didn't. There were no hospitals in those days.

Miss, my Auntie Brenda had to go to the hospital.

Well, Mary didn't. Now just listen, there's a good boy. My goodness, we will never get through the story with all these interruptions. Joseph looked everywhere for somewhere to stay. He asked at the inn but the innkeeper said that there was no room. There was only the stable where the ox and the ass slept.

Miss, what's an ass?

It's a donkey, Briony.

I wouldn't like to sleep with a donkey, Miss. The one in Blackpool was really smelly and tried to kick my dad and bite his hand.

Dean, this was a very nice donkey in the stable. Soon Mary would have her very special baby and lay him in swaddling clothes in a manger.

The donkeys in Blackpool were mangy, Miss. My dad said.

I said manger, Dean, not mangy. The Angel told Mary not to fear. He brought tidings of great joy, but he told Joseph to take Mary and the baby and flee to Egypt.

Miss, the donkeys in Blackpool had fleas, Miss. My Auntie Christine was scratching the whole holiday and . . .

I think we will finish the story tomorrow, children. Now, sit up smartly, nice straight backs, eyes this way, and we will wait for the bell.

My Dad Remembers

When I was a lad I walked to school
In pouring rain and freezing sleet,
With satchel crammed with heavy books,
I trekked for miles with aching feet . . .
But I was happy!

When I was a lad I shared a bed
In a room with bare boards on the floor.
No central heating, double glazing,
We didn't even have a door . . .
But I was happy!

When I was a lad I had no toys,
Computers, TVs and the like.
You were thought to be a millionaire
If you owned a football or a bike . . .
But I was happy!

When I was a lad, food was scarce,
I licked the pattern off the plate.
We never saw an ice-cream cone,
A bag of sweets or chocolate cake . . .
But I was happy!

When I was a lad, school was strict
And teachers hit you with a cane
Just for speaking out in class.
I never opened my mouth again . . .
But I was happy!

I remember well that golden age.
The memories make me feel quite sad.
Why, every day was a holiday,
In the good old days when I was a lad!

In the Queue

'You, boy!' barked the teacher
to the pupil at the back of the queue.
'Why are you whistling?'
'Sir,' replied the boy, 'because I'm happy!'

Telling Teacher

Miss, Peter's pinched my pencil.

Miss, Sally's in my seat.

Miss, Mandy's making noises.

Miss, William's work's not neat.

Miss, Simon's being silly.

Miss, Paula's took my pen.

Miss, Frankie's pulling faces.

Miss, Leroy's late again.

Miss, Cheryl-Ann is chewing.

Miss, Patrick's pulled my hair.

Miss, Elizabeth's not listening.

Miss, Tamsin's took my chair.

Miss, Dan's not done his homework.

Miss, Kevin's killed a bee.

Miss, Natalie's being naughty –

And Miss – why will no one play with me ?

Cat and Dog

One bright morning,
The kitten,
Exploring the garden,
Found the dozing dog stretched on the path in the sun.
The cat,
Cautious, curious,
Watched for a while.
Then,
Slowly, silently
(First one paw, then the other)
It padded closer,
Purring softly.
Then
It pounced!
Ah, playful kitten,
You have learnt
Life's early lessons:
Let sleeping dogs lie,
Once bitten, twice shy.

Conversation with the Parent

May I have a biscuit, Mum?
If you say the magic word.
Abracadabra!

Star Turn

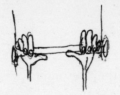

'You see those men,' said Uncle Ken,
'Whose arms stretch past their knees,
Who drag their knuckles across the floor
Like two great chimpanzees?
Well, they're the stars of the Circus –
The Men on the Flying Trapeze!'

A Word of Warning!

Here's a word of warning
For every mother's son
Who thinks that he is quick enough
Across the road to run,

When heavily laden lorries,
And swaying caravans,
Race down the road at rush hour,
With buses, cars and vans,

Who thinks that he can make it
Across the carriageway,
And ignores the zebra crossing
A hundred yards away,

Who thinks that he is quicker
Than a cow in a stampede,
That he can run much faster
Than a motorbike at speed.

Well, here's word of warning,
For every mother's son,
Who thinks that he is quick enough
Across the road to run.

DON'T!

Mother Said

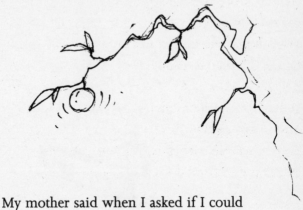

My mother said when I asked if I could
have another peach,
'They don't grow on trees, you know!'

Brother Said

My brother said: 'When I was your age I never
behaved as you do!'
He sounds more like my father every day!

As You Were

Soft as fur, hard as iron,
Timid as a mouse, brave as a lion.
Weak as water, strong as an ox,
Round as a ring, square as a box.
Lazy as a lizard, busy as a bee,
High as the mountains, deep as the sea.
Dead as a doornail, live as a wire,
Cold as an iceberg, hot as fire.
Bright as sunshine, dull as a stone,
Wet as a raindrop, dry as a bone.
Heavy as lead, light as a feather,
Smooth as silk, tough as old leather.
Small as an ant, big as a whale,
Fast as a ferret, slow as a snail.
Thin as a beanpole, thick as a rope,
Safe as houses, slippery as soap.
Dark as a mineshaft, clear as light,
Loud as thunder, quiet as the night.
Happy as Dad and happy as Mum,
Happy as me when the holidays come!

Angel in the Cloakroom

Last week, when I was looking for my
PE kit in the cloakroom,
I saw an angel.
She was hovering above the coat
hooks, smiling at me
And waving a long white hand.
Her silver wings were trembling
And her golden halo shimmered in the sun.
This morning she was there again,
Smiling and shimmering,
Flapping and fluttering,
Waving and trembling.
She looked beautiful.

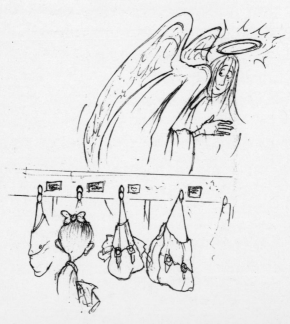

I told my teacher.
'Miss, there's an angel in the cloakroom.'
My teacher gave a little snort. 'An angel?'
She looked around the cloakroom but the
angel had gone.
'Too much television,' she sighed.
'Too lively an imagination.
A daydreamer, that's what you are.
Angels indeed. Whatever next?'
She smiled and shook her head,
And then picked up a shining feather
from the floor
And put it in the bin.

Becky's Tree

When Becky died, we planted a tree
At the front of the school.
A small, straight sapling it was,
Thin as a stick with delicate branches,
And a pale, smooth bark.
It looked so sad and bare
That cold, dark autumn day,
When we said a prayer and cried.
It reminded us of Becky
When she became ill:
Lean and white and tired-looking.

In winter the little tree looked dead,
Standing stiff and lifeless in the snow.
But in the spring the slender branches
Burst with fat green buds
And then with glistening leaves.
On one sunny morning we left our books
And stared in silence from the classroom window
At Becky's tree, draped in silver blossom.
It was so beautiful. We cried
And we remembered Becky.

Up the Stairs

'Who is that shouting at the top of the stairs?'
Shouted the teacher.
'Who is that shouting at the bottom of the stairs?'
Came a pupil's reply.

Dreaming

In the corner of the classroom,
A small child stared at the stuffed hedgehog
In the glass case.
'What are you thinking of?' asked the school inspector.
'I was just wondering,' the child replied wistfully,
'What it was doing . . . before it was stuffed!'

Spelling

The inspector asked the little ones,
'Can anyone tell me,
A word that begins with the letter 'Q'?'
And a child said, 'Quistmas twee!'

The Song of the School Inspector

What shall we do with the school inspector?
What shall we do with the school inspector?
What shall we do with the school inspector?
Early in the morning.

Stand him by the gate when the school bell's ringing,
Stand him by the gate when the school bell's ringing,
Stand him by the gate when the school bell's ringing,
Early in the morning.

Oh, see the teachers rushing,
Oh, feel the pupils pushing,
Oh dear! The queues are crushing,
Early in the morning.

What shall we do with the school inspector?
What shall we do with the school inspector?
What shall we do with the school inspector?
Early in the morning.

Sit him on the stage in the school assembly,
Sit him on the stage in the school assembly,
Sit him on the stage in the school assembly,
Early in the morning.

Oh dear, it's oh so boring,
Oh dear, someone's snoring,
Now hear the teachers roaring,
Early in the morning.

What shall we do with the school inspector?
What shall we do with the school inspector?
What shall we do with the school inspector?
Early in the morning.

Put him in the classroom to watch the teachers,
Put him in the classroom to watch the teachers,
Put him in the classroom to watch the teachers,
Early in the morning.

Oh, look, I see him prying,
Oh dear, I see him spying,
Oh, hear the teachers crying,
Early in the morning.

What shall we do with the school inspector?
What shall we do with the school inspector?
What shall we do with the school inspector?
Early in the morning.

Let him have his lunch with the infant children,
Let him have his lunch with the infant children,
Let him have his lunch with the infant children,
Early in the morning.

Oh dear, he looks quite prickly,
Oh dear, that child feels sickly,
Oh dear, his suit's all sticky,
Early in the morning.

What shall we do with the school inspector?
What shall we do with the school inspector?
What shall we do with the school inspector?
Early in the morning.

Put him in the playground when it's snowing,
Put him in the playground when it's snowing,
Put him in the playground when it's snowing,
Early in the morning.

Oh dear, I hear his sneezing,
Oh dear, I hear him wheezing,
Oh dear, his hands are freezing,
Early in the morning.

What shall we do with the school inspector?
What shall we do with the school inspector?
What shall we do with the school inspector?
Early in the morning.

Lock him in the cupboard when the school day's over,
Lock him in the cupboard when the school day's over,
Lock him in the cupboard when the school day's over,
Early in the morning.

Oh, can you hear him tapping?
Oh, how he's madly rapping,
I hear the teachers clapping,
Until early the next morning.

Baking

'We've been baking in class today,
Would you like my last jam tart?
It's funny how clean my hands are now.
They were dirty at the start!'

Lament

On Monday I found a wasps' nest in my garden,
Pale brown and thin as paper –
An oval husk.
I carried it carefully to school to show my teacher.
'Very nice, Richard,' said Miss Smout.
'Pop it on my desk, dear, and we will look at it later.'
But we never did.

On Tuesday I found a feather in the gutter,
Deep purple and as soft as snow –
A delicate dart.
I carried it carefully to school to show my teacher.
'Very nice, Richard,' said Miss Smout.
'Pop it on my desk, dear, and we will look at it later.'
But we never did.

On Wednesday I found a pebble in the playground.
Speckled green and hard as ice –
A dragon's egg.
I carried it carefully into school to show my teacher.
'Very nice, Richard,' said Miss Smout.
'Pop it on my desk, dear, and we will look at it later.'
But we never did.

On Thursday I found a key beneath the wall,
Rusty red and cold as winter –
A dungeon opener.
I carried it carefully into school to show my teacher.
'Very nice, Richard,' said Miss Smout.
'Pop it on my desk, dear, and we will look at it later.'
But we never did.

On Friday I found a worksheet on my desk,
Long and white and with bold black print –
A tombstone.
I filled in all the blanks and carried it carefully
to show my teacher.
'Very nice, Richard,' said Miss Smout.
'Pop it on my desk, dear, and we will look at it later.'
And unfortunately – we did.

The Sweet-shop Rap

If you go down to the shops today,
And you pop in the sweet shop on the way,
Well, sing out loud and dance and clap,
And all join in to this sweet-shop rap.

You gotta chew, chew, suck and munch,
Chomp and gnaw and nibble and crunch,
Sing and shout and dance and clap,
Just tap your feet to the sweet-shop rap.

There's butterscotch and lemon drops,
Candyfloss and lollipops,
Gobstoppers, humbugs, icing-sugar mice,
You just make your choice and pay the price.

You gotta chew, chew, suck and munch,
Chomp and gnaw and nibble and crunch,
Sing and shout and dance and clap,
Just tap your feet to the sweet-shop rap.

There's jelly babies and bubble gum,
Aniseed balls and sugared plum,
Sticky toffee crammed in jars,
Marshmallow, fudge and marzipan bars.

You gotta chew, chew, suck and munch,
Chomp and gnaw and nibble and crunch,
Sing and shout and dance and clap,
Just tap your feet to the sweet-shop rap.

There's dolly mixtures, sherbet dips,
Easter eggs and chocolate whips,
Nougat, bullseyes, seaside rock,
Just take your pick from the sweet-shop stock.

You gotta chew, chew, suck and munch,
Chomp and gnaw and nibble and crunch,
Sing and shout and dance and clap,
Just tap your feet to the sweet-shop rap.

Mint imperials, liquorice whirls,
Coconut squares and caramel curls.
There's every sort of sweet confection,
So don't delay – make your selection.

You gotta chew, chew, suck and munch,
Chomp and gnaw and nibble and crunch,
Sing and shout and dance and clap,
Just tap your feet to the sweet-shop rap.

But wait a minute – stop this rap!
If you eat all those sweets you'll get very very fat,
And you'll certainly scream and squeal and shout,
And splutter and spit when your teeth fall out.

So don't chew, chew, suck and munch,
Don't chomp and gnaw and nibble and crunch,
Don't sing out loud and dance and clap,
Let that be the end of the sweet-shop rap.

And that's that!

I'm Not Scared

I'm not scared of vampire bats,
Growling wolves and hissing cats.
I'm not scared of snarling dogs,
Slippery slugs and jumping frogs,
And dancing shadows on the wall,
Well, they don't bother me at all!

I'm not scared of slimy snails,
Whistling winds and howling gales.
I'm not scared of trembling quakes,
Hairy spiders, hissing snakes,
And ferocious pirates in a crowd,
Well, they just make me laugh out loud!

I'm not scared of stinging bees,
Wriggly worms and itchy fleas.
I'm not scared of darkened rooms,
Cackling witches on their brooms,
And sharp-toothed monsters of the deep,
Well, they will send me off to sleep!

I'm not scared of grizzly bears,
Hospitals and dentist's chairs,
Hurricanes and lightning flashes,
Tornadoes, whirlwinds, thunder crashes.
None of these give me a fright,
But Mummy, don't turn out the light!

Our Cat Cuddles

Mum and Dad said one day: Would you like a kitten?
We could get one from
the RSPCA.

I said: I'd like a fat cat, a fierce cat,
A ferocious catch-a-rat cat.

Mum said: I'd like a furry cat, a fluffy cat,
A friendly sit-on-your-lap cat.

Dad said: I'd like a sleek cat, a meek cat,
A lazy, sleep-at-your-feet cat.

Lizzie said: I don't mind, whatever kind
Will be all right for me.

So one bright sunny summer's day
We visited the RSPCA.
And at the pound, to our surprise,
Were animals of every shape and size.
Foxes, ferrets, pheasants, bats,
Terrapins, turtles, weasels, rats,
Hamsters, hedgehogs, snakes and voles,
Pigeons, parrots, mice and moles,
Horses, donkeys, newts and frogs,
Ducks and drakes and cats and dogs,
Rabbits, lizards, otters, owls,
Gerbils, goldfish, guinea-fowls,
Beavers, badgers, squirrels, stoats,
Swans and sheep and billy-goats.

We'd like a kitten, please, Dad said.
The keeper smiled and scratched his head.
What sort of cat have you in mind?
We've every colour and every kind.

I said: I'd like a fierce cat, a fat cat
                 A ferocious, catch-a-rat cat.

The keeper said: We've got tabby cats, shabby cats,
                 Wild cats, mild cats,
                 Creeping cats, sleeping cats,
                 Prowling cats, growling cats,
                 City cats, witty cats,
                 Lazy cats, crazy cats,
                 Shy cats, sly cats,
                 Spit-you-in-the-eye cats.

Mum said: I'd like a furry cat, a fluffy cat,
                 A friendly, sit-on-your-lap cat.

The keeper said: We've got white cats, night cats,
Dancing cats, prancing cats,
Slim cats, trim cats,
Lanky cats, swanky cats,
Frizzy cats, dizzy cats,
Moody cats, broody cats,
Lean cats, mean cats,
Very, very clean cats.

Dad said: I'd like a sleek cat, a meek cat,
A lazy, sleep-at-your-feet cat.

The keeper said: We've got grey cats, stray cats,
Hissing cats, kissing cats,
Fair cats, rare cats,
Grumpy cats, lumpy cats,
Old cats, bold cats,
Slender cats, tender cats,
Town cats, brown cats,
Jumping-up-and-down cats.

We looked in every cage and then
We came upon a wire pen,
And in the corner all alone,
There curled a kitten – skin and bone,
With great sad eyes and matted fur,
We heard its faint pathetic purr.
Lizzie clapped her hands in glee,
'That kitten is the one for me!'
We called him Cuddles and took him home,
Since then he's grown and grown and grown.

I say: It sits in the sun and growls all day,
            Then chases all my friends away.

Mum says: It's scratched the curtains into shreds,
            It's ripped the sheets on all the beds.

Dad says: It's gnawed the table, chomped the chairs,
            It's chewed the carpet on the stairs.

Well, I don't care, said Little Liz,
I like him just the way he is.
He's now got fangs and massive paws,
A shaggy mane and sharp, sharp claws,
Great golden eyes and rumbling growl,
A long brown tail and fearsome howl.
But we've had to change his name to Brian.
Because Cuddles does not suit a lion!

Interview with the Headmaster

Headmaster: Why are you here outside my room, boy?

Pupil: Mr Pounder sent me out of class, Sir.

Headmaster: Sent you out!

Pupil: Yes, Sir. He told me to wait outside your room.

Headmaster: Did he?

Pupil: Yes, Sir.

Headmaster: Why did Mr Pounder send you out?

Pupil: Gross insolence, Sir.

Headmaster: Gross insolence?

Pupil: Yes, Sir

Headmaster: You've been sent out for gross insolence?

Pupil: That's right, Sir.

Headmaster: This sounds very serious.

Pupil: Yes, Sir.

Headmaster: What did you say, boy?

Pupil: I didn't say anything, Sir.

Headmaster: What do you mean you didn't say anything?

Pupil: I didn't say anything, Sir.

Headmaster: How can you be grossly insolent if you did not say anything?

Pupil: I wrote it down, Sir.

Headmaster: You wrote it down?

Pupil: Yes, Sir. We were asked to write an essay.

Headmaster: An essay?

Pupil: Yes, Sir.

Headmaster: What sort of essay?

Pupil: A long essay, Sir.

Headmaster: And what was the title of this long essay?

Pupil: Imagine you are a new-born baby and describe your first week in the world, Sir.

Headmaster: And?

Pupil: And I wrote three pages, Sir.

Headmaster: And?

Pupil: I was sent out, Sir.

Headmaster: What did you write, boy?

Pupil: Glug, glug, glug, glug, glug . . . Sir.

Lizzie's Spider

When Lizzie was a little girl,
A tiny tot of three,
She found a spider in the hall,
It crawled up on her knee.
Eight hairy legs the spider had,
And a body like a pea,
And little Lizzie picked it up,
And held it tenderly.

When Lizzie was a little girl,
A tiny tot of three,
Each day she'd go into the hall,
That spider for to see.
She'd watch it spin its silvery web
Of finest filigree,
And little Lizzie picked it up,
And held it tenderly.

When Lizzie was a little girl,
A tiny tot of three,
She took the spider from the hall,
Her mother for to see,
And found her in the kitchen,
Busy making tea.
'What have you there?' her mother asked,
'Oh, Lizzie, let me see.'

103

When Lizzie was a little girl,
A tiny tot of three,
She opened wide her little hands,
And smiled in child-like glee,
And showed her mother what she held
So very tenderly.
Mummy shot out of the kitchen
Like a squirrel up a tree.

Now Lizzie, she is all grown up,
And a happy girl is she,
But she's terrified of spiders.
Now – why ever should that be?

When I Grow Up

'When I grow up,' Elizabeth said, 'a PRINCESS I will be,
With a crown on my head and a cloak of red
And the crowds will stare at me.
But I am rather shy,' she said with a sigh,
'so that won't do for me!'

'When I grow up,' Elizabeth said, 'an ASTRONAUT I'll be.
And I'll spin through space with a smile on my face
And be back in time for tea.
But I think I would cry so high in the sky,
so that won't do for me!'

'When I grow up,' Elizabeth said, 'a SAILOR I will be.
And I'll ride the gale on a great white whale
When I swim away to sea.
But I get very sick when I sail in a ship,
so that won't do for me!'

'When I grow up,' Elizabeth said, 'an EXPLORER I will be.
In a jungle dank, I'll sit on a bank
With a tiger on my knee.
But I might get a scratch from that great big cat,
so that won't do for me!'

'When I grow up,' Elizabeth said, 'an *ARTIST* I will be.
And I'll draw and I'll etch and I'll paint and I'll sketch
Everything I see.
But the smell of paint will make me feel faint,
so that won't do for me!'

'When I grow up,' Elizabeth said, 'a *MILLIONAIRE* I'll be.
And I'll lock every pound in a chest in the ground
And hide away the key.
But I might not recall where I've hidden it all,
so that won't do for me!'

'When I grow up,' Elizabeth said,
'I know just what I'll be.
I'll be like my mum and have lots of fun
Looking after a girl like *ME*!'

When Lizzie Was Born

When Lizzie was born, Dad called the brothers
(aged nine and seven and five)
Into the kitchen and announced grandly:
'You have a baby sister.'
He smiled like a fat-faced frog which had caught a fly.
The boys looked deeply unimpressed.
'We thought that it would be a boy,' said Richard,
Accompanied by his brothers' serious nods.
'Well, it's not,' said Dad.
'It is a little baby girl,
And she is beautiful, oh so beautiful.'
'Will she make a lot of noise?' asked Matthew.
'I guess she will,' said Dad.
'All babies do.
You did.'

'And will she smell?' asked Dominic.
'I guess she will do that as well,' said Dad,
'All babies do.
You did.'
'You are quite sure it is a girl?' asked Richard,
His brow furrowing.
'Quite sure,' said Dad and sighed.
'And she's so beautiful, oh so beautiful:
Pink and soft, with hair like liquid gold,
And tiny fingernails like polished shells,
And little toes like pearly buds,
And delicate ears and dainty button nose,
And such a smile, oh, such a smile.'
'Please don't go on,' said Richard, holding up a hand,
'I'm sure she's very nice.'
Then, turning to his brothers, he remarked,
'I suppose we'll just have to get used to the idea.'

Golden Grannies

Once when my dad was mad with me
For not tidying my bedroom,
Stabbing the air with a bony finger
And raising the roof with his shouts,
Grandma, who was sitting behind him at the time,
Pulled a funny face and stuck out her tongue.
I started to grin and giggle, smile, then splutter.
Dad, crimson-faced, ballooning with anger,
Was, for once, completely lost for words.
Then, seeing Grandma's manic face in the mirror,
He turned and cried: 'Mother!
I am trying to instil some discipline here!
You are not really helping!'

'Oh do shut up!' said Grandma quietly.
'Leave the lad alone.
He's only little, bless him.
Your bedroom was not a palace when you were young.
In fact it looked as if a bomb had hit it,
And I never ever told you off,
Or shouted so at you or wagged a finger thus.
There are more important things in life
than an untidy room.
Now, go and put the kettle on.
I could do with a cup of tea.'
Grannies! They are worth their weight in gold!

Alphabet of Love

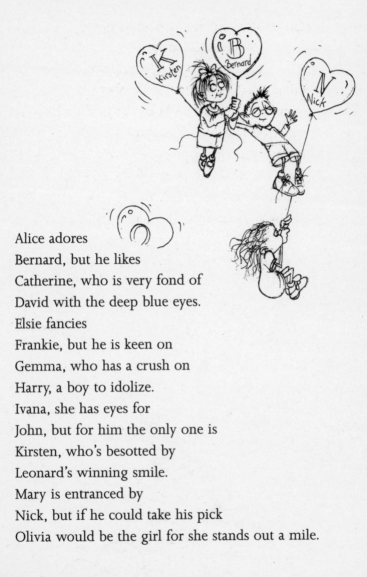

Alice adores
Bernard, but he likes
Catherine, who is very fond of
David with the deep blue eyes.
Elsie fancies
Frankie, but he is keen on
Gemma, who has a crush on
Harry, a boy to idolize.
Ivana, she has eyes for
John, but for him the only one is
Kirsten, who's besotted by
Leonard's winning smile.
Mary is entranced by
Nick, but if he could take his pick
Olivia would be the girl for she stands out a mile.

Peter yearns for

Queenie, but she is quite devoted to

Ronald, who's completely smitten by

Samantha's golden curls.

Terry is just wild about

Ulrika with the little pout, but she dotes on

Vincent, who chases all the girls.

Wendy worships

Xavier, who is very keen on

Yelda, but she's in love for all to see with lonely little

Zebedee.

Last Word

'Every time I open my mouth,'
Shouted the teacher,
'Some idiot speaks!'

Index of First Lines